BULLDOGS

Valerie Bodden

Creative Education

published by Creative Education
P.O. Box 227, Mankato, Minnesota 56002
Creative Education is an imprint of
The Creative Company
www.thecreativecompany.us

design and production by
Christine Vanderbeek
art direction by Rita Marshall
printed in the United States of America

photographs by by Alamy (AF archive,
Mary Evans Picture Library, Moviestore
collection Ltd, Tierfotoagentur), Dreamstime
(Isselee), iStockphoto (Richard Clark, Eric
Isselée, Tetiana Katsai, rusm), Mary Evans
Picture Library (Ronald Grant Archive),
Shutterstock (Justin Black, Eric Isselee, Erik
Lam, Neveshkin Nikolay, Viorel Sima, Katsai
Tatiana, Nikolai Tsvetkov, WilleeCole)

library of congress
cataloging-in-publication data
Bodden, Valerie.
Bulldogs / Valerie Bodden.
p. cm. — (Fetch!)
SUMMARY: A brief overview of the physical
characteristics, personality traits, and habits
of the bulldog breed, as well as descriptions
of famous pop-culture bulldogs such as Bull
the Bulldog.
Includes index.

ISBN 978-1-60818-361-6
1. Bulldog—Juvenile literature. I. Title.
SF429.B85B63 2014
636.72—dc23   2013005515

first edition
9 8 7 6 5 4 3 2 1

TABLE OF CONTENTS

Loving Bulldogs   **5**

What Do Bulldogs Look Like?   **6**

Bulldog Puppies   **10**

Bulldogs in Cartoons   **13**

Bulldogs and People   **14**

What Do Bulldogs Like to Do?   **18**

A Famous Bulldog   **23**

Glossary **24** • Read More **24** • Websites **24** • Index **24**

LOVING BULLDOGS

A bulldog is a *breed* of dog. Bulldogs look tough. But they are gentle and loving. They are playful dogs that like to clown around.

WHAT DO BULLDOGS LOOK LIKE?

Bulldogs have wide bodies and big heads. They have wrinkly faces. Bulldogs have short ears and short tails. French bulldogs have ears that stand up straight.

English (above) and French (right) bulldogs have smooth coats.

Fetch!

French bulldogs are the smallest kind of bulldogs. They weigh less than 30 pounds (14 kg). English bulldogs are a little taller than a ruler. They weigh 40 to 50 pounds (18–23 kg). American bulldogs are taller. They can weigh up to 120 pounds (54 kg). All bulldogs have short fur. The fur can be red, yellowish brown, or white. Or it can be more than one color.

Even young American bulldogs are bigger than English and French bulldogs.

BULLDOG PUPPIES

Most newborn bulldog puppies weigh less than one pound (0.5 kg). The puppies grow quickly. Soon they begin to run around. They can be clumsy!

A mother bulldog has four to seven puppies at a time.

BULLDOGS IN CARTOONS

Bulldogs can be seen in many cartoons. Hector the Bulldog appears in Looney Tunes cartoons. He keeps Tweety Bird safe from Sylvester the Cat. In *Tom and Jerry*, Tom the cat gets in trouble with Spike the bulldog.

Jerry the mouse was good at making Spike get mad at Tom.

BULLDOGS AND PEOPLE

About 800 years ago, people in England began to use bulldogs for **bull baiting**. The bulldogs had to bite a bull on its nose. Bull baiting was made **illegal** more than 150 years ago. American and French bulldogs are **descended** from bulldogs in England.

Bull baiting was not safe for bulldogs or bulls.

Bulldogs are good with kids. Bulldog puppies can make good pets. They are cute and active. Adult bulldogs can make good pets, too. But French bulldog adults might have a hard time getting used to kids. Both male and female bulldogs make good pets.

Pet bulldogs will be their owner's friends forever.

WHAT DO BULLDOGS LIKE TO DO?

English and French bulldogs do not need a lot of exercise. But American bulldogs need to get some exercise every day. Bulldogs need to be brushed two or three times a week. Their face wrinkles need to be washed often.

Many bulldogs like to sleep more than they like to run.

Fetch!

Bulldogs love to spend time with their owners. Take your bulldog for a short walk. Then go inside and curl up together. You will both have fun!

A FAMOUS BULLDOG

Bull is an English bulldog in the Walt Disney movie *Lady and the Tramp.* At the beginning of the movie, Bull is in the back of a dogcatcher's truck. But Tramp unlocks the truck to let Bull escape. Later, Bull is in the dog pound when Lady is brought there. He talks to her about Tramp.

GLOSSARY

breed a kind of an animal with certain traits, such as long ears or a good nose

bull baiting a sport in which people watched bulldogs bite and hang on to a chained bull's nose

descended related to a person or animal that lived in the past

illegal against the law

READ MORE

Frisch, Joy. *Bulldogs*. North Mankato, Minn.: Smart Apple Media, 2004.

Green, Sara. *Bulldogs*. Minneapolis: Bellwether Media, 2010.

Johnson, Jinny. *Bulldog*. North Mankato, Minn.: Smart Apple Media, 2013.

WEBSITES

Bailey's Responsible Dog Owner's Coloring Book
http://classic.akc.org/pdfs/public_education/coloring_book.pdf
Print out pictures to color, and learn more about caring for a pet dog.

Just Dog Breeds: Bulldog
http://www.www.justdogbreeds.com/bulldog.html
Learn more about bulldogs and check out lots of bulldog pictures.

Every effort has been made to ensure that these sites are suitable for children, that they have educational value, and that they contain no inappropriate material. However, because of the nature of the Internet, it is impossible to guarantee that these sites will remain active indefinitely or that their contents will not be altered.

INDEX

bodies 6
brushing 18
bull baiting 14
Bull the Bulldog 23

cartoons 13
exercise 18, 21
fur 9
heads 6

puppies 10, 17
sizes 9
tails 6
wrinkles 6, 18